EXPLORING THE CONCEPT OF WANDERLUST

HARPER NORTHWOOD

CONTENTS

1 Introduction to Wanderlust   1

2 The Psychology of Wanderlust   5

3 Smart Travel Planning   9

4 Cultural Immersion and Deep Connections   13

5 Adventure and Bold Living   17

6 Sustainable Travel Practices   21

7 Digital Nomadism and Remote Work   25

8 Solo Travel and Group Dynamics   29

9 Traveling with Purpose   33

10 Health and Wellness on the Road   37

11 Capturing Memories and Storytelling   41

12 Reflections on Wanderlust and Personal Growth   45

CHAPTER 1

Introduction to Wanderlust

The word *wanderlust*, with its pedestrian roots in German, has recently infiltrated the English language to become a captivating metaphor used to express a yearning for faraway places, a keenness for roaming and adventure, and a pronounced affection for unrestrained exploration of the world. For the first time in human history, people all over the world share this intense desire to see and know the world, frequently and largely unabatedly. Ancient explorers and frontiersmen braved the perils of the surface world to secure a better tomorrow, driven by a longing to reach the ends of the globe. Instead of seeking mere survival, they sought inspiration, appreciating the journey as much as the desired destination.

This yearning may be derived from specific holiday recollections that filled us with excitement rather than escape. Alternatively, it can be a visual representation of a quest to conquer a lengthy journey, see everything on your must-see roster, and celebrate every aspect of it. In modern times, 'travel' signifies embarking on a new adventure. It has become a significant aspect of the psychological economy, with many traveling to realize dreams that lurk just beneath the veneer of their restrictive daily lives. The journey itself becomes as significant as the goal. To fill your wanderlust cravings, you don't necessarily need to go on any trips or see typical points of interest. This book pertains to both regular and leisurely travel, providing insights into how travel offers a new narrative for our lives.

The irony of life is paradoxically comforting and refreshing when you find yourself in strange surroundings. While traveling, you might experience a significant mid-life existential crisis, realizing that wanderlust isn't just about vacationing. It's about deepening the relationship within yourself and living deeply and bravely.

Defining Wanderlust

Wanderlust manifests as an intense urge to explore the world. For some, it appears as dreams of hop-scotching across the globe; for others, it is a dull ache for adventure. This longing to see new formations of water, fresh skylines, exotic flavors, and unique faces comes with a deep whiff of romance. Wanderlust offers not just thrills but happiness, not just connection with customs but also with oneself. It has a name, this complex feeling of desire and anxiety, this mix of longing and experience: wanderlust.

This dual understanding of wanderlust – as a search for what we don't have at home and as the pursuit of a felt absence – embodies the emotional entanglement with the concept. Wanderlust suggests that it may entail alternative worlds and a sense that longing is fulfilled elsewhere. The significance of places, landscapes, and cultures experienced on the road is felt anew upon returning home. Thus, while wanderlust feeds on dreams of consumption and desire, travel becomes much more than a stage for the completion of fantasy or the fulfillment of dreams.

Historically, a longing for travel and the exotic was absent for most of human history. Although some people journeyed for trade, others migrated, and still others left home as refugees, travelers and migrants were typically looked down upon in traditional agrarian societies where people tended to stay close to home. As long as travel was looked down upon, a longing to wander remained the longing of cultural outsiders who set themselves apart due to their disdain for convention and social pressure. As the urban middle class grew and modernized, travel for pleasure became more acceptable, but the longing to travel continued to stand in contrast to home. Today, wanderlust represents choice rather than necessity, designating a certain privileged attitude, lifestyle, and fantasy about the individual and social self.

Historical and Cultural Perspectives

In *Wandering: A Cultural History of Walking*, Solnit traces the shift in public opinion toward wayfarers: "Dislocation, from the land and its rituals and the many kinds of tied-known's that brings, comes to connote a shattering, a theft. These rootless boys and girls haunt vicinity with their hobo amorality. They became – stereotypically – demoralized." The sacred peripetia was dismissed as part of humanity, and wanderlust began to be separated between the mere compulsion to roam and an armchair escape breeding deviance from society.

Historically, the symptoms of wanderlust were considered pathological, stemming from a profound and solitary madness. The origins of this early understanding of wanderlust appear to have been embedded in the basic emotional responses triggered by travel. Samuel Johnson spoke of travel as a personal emotion of "Keh-keh-keh!" and Brissot de Warville warned the French, "Gare au voyage: C'est dans le bonheur du voyageur que se tient le malheur du paysan [Watch out for travelers, for the happiness of the voyager causes the misery of the peasant]."

Viewing wanderlust from a historical and cultural perspective also helps explain many of the psychological and sociological approaches to wanderlust, at least in national Western cultures. The word "wanderlust" has not done the same in other languages, remaining in this conceptual ghetto, carrying both connotations of yearning and pathology.

The social context has provided foundations for the notion of wanderlust. From a broader societal view, one could argue that the Genesis account of the expulsion of Adam and Eve from the Garden marked a shift from animals wandering in the wild to humans with substantial purpose.

CHAPTER 2

The Psychology of Wanderlust

Psychologists define *wanderlust*, or the intense desire to travel, as an attempt at self-exploration and a sense of freedom, rather than a form of escapism. While many find themselves drawn to exploring new destinations and cultures, psychologists and researchers have sought to understand the underlying motivations and drivers of our desires to travel. Professor Ruth Ann Atchley at the University of Kansas coined the term "rusty wanderers" to describe people who spend years in the same environment while still feeling wanderlust. Our consistent motivation to explore and travel is largely fueled by the range of new experiences we seek. As we familiarize ourselves with our often homogenous surroundings, our brains stagnate, and our levels of stimulation and engagement consequently decrease. By changing our environment and exploring new cultures, we re-engage with the world around us, making travel an essential mechanism for staying sharp and curious.

This deeper understanding of wanderlust also allows us to comprehend its related emotions. As humans, our natural tendency is to adapt to novel experiences. This process, known as "hedonic adaptation," is the body's way of regulating the effects of positive and negative emotions, filtering experiences into our backgrounds as we get used to them, similar to an artist shading subjects to 'fade' into the surrounding background. While this psychological tool may create happiness and optimization, it also desensitizes us to stimulus over time. In the context of wanderlust, we come to expect many of these new experiences as a natural part of our lives, which is why it is sometimes seen as a form of escapism. Only by shifting our mindset away from this escapist orientation can we unlock a sense of active exploration and fulfillment when heading on a journey.

Motivations and Drivers

The wanderlust lifestyle is motivated by a combination of desires to see new landscapes, meet new people, and learn about different ways of being. The benefits of travel are well-documented, so we need not delve into why people desire to see new places—instead, our concern is with the social and emotional desires that drive this urge. People decide they want to travel for various reasons. In many cases, young people are propelled across the world, away from the familiarity of home, because their lives are filled with uncertainty. Those adolescent and post-adolescent years are when we are most concerned with making personal choices. In response to this uncertainty, a dualistic dialectic is pursued.

One projection in our attempt to make sense of the entrapment faced by contemporary humans paints us as rootless and directionless travelers driven by familiar cultural shapers—capitalism, consumerism, technology, Thomas Cook, Lonely Planet. These external forces are deeply ingrained in society and have shaped values, goals, and motivations in ways such that travelers no longer think for themselves and fear the individual freedom and self-responsibility that would come about if they dared to think apart from the crowd. This ceaseless irony of uncertainty is the central paradox that underpins this chapter: humans hate the concept of feeling uncertain, yet they embrace it as an excuse to define their very being. In modern Western society, this uncertainty propels young people across the world in search of personal 'unforgettability,' individuality, and unadulterated experience. These endeavors lead to the discovery of oneself and provide a sense of direction and purpose in life.

Benefits and Drawbacks

Wanderlust allows people to see more in a day than many see in a year. As the incurable desire to travel and see the world, wanderlust has its benefits. Wanderers are not just tourists; they experience and enter the worlds they pass through in ways that enrich their perspective and worldview. At the same time, wanderlust has drawbacks, as the intense desire to keep moving and exploring can make it difficult to stay in one place and put down roots. Whether it is a chronic challenge for some or a brief emotional and mental longing, wanderlust has its benefits and drawbacks.

Benefits:

- **Experiencing Life:** Although wanderlust is often associated with a love for travel and exploring, a defining aspect is the desire and ambition to experience new things, embrace opportunities, accept the unknown, and challenge oneself. Those who embrace wanderlust want to make the most out of every moment.
- **Broadening Perspectives:** Wanderlust enriches one's perspective by exposing individuals to different cultures, lifestyles, and worldviews, thereby fostering a broader understanding of humanity.

Drawbacks:

- **Challenges in Settling Down:** The urge to keep moving and exploring can present challenges in relationships and professional life, requiring security and commitment to one organization or institution.
- **Fear of Missing Out:** The overwhelming desire to move and experience can lead to fear of missing out and regret, particularly at a young age.

By recognizing both the advantages and disadvantages of wanderlust, individuals can navigate their desires to explore with a balanced approach, ensuring that their journey through life is as fulfilling as possible.

CHAPTER 3

Smart Travel Planning

One of the most important road signs for living a bold life is the concept of smart travel. Living a bold life often entails living a life on the road, embracing unconventional adventures, thoughtful preparation, and making choices that support your travel goals. Smart travel does not mean a quick weekend getaway, two weeks in a sunshine-soaked location, or working your way through the top ten destinations in your travel guide. Instead, smart travel means embarking on thoughtful and well-planned journeys that enrich your experiences and expand your horizons.

Strategies for Smart Travel

For many, travel is a dream reserved for the rich, retired, or those looking to escape the daily grind. But here's the truth: traveling the world is possible for anyone. Wanderlust isn't just for the wealthy or the beautiful. Of course, money helps, and jobs that take you to places like Vietnam or Sweden have their benefits. However, the essence of DIY (Do-It-Yourself) travel planning lies in understanding that smart travel is the result of good travel planning. Before you go anywhere, you must make decisions about how you'll travel, who you'll travel with, and what you'll do when you get there.

Research and Preparation: The decision to travel, where to go, and what to do are critical moments in advance of any journey. Research and planning are key components at this initial phase. The direction a person selects can tell a great deal about who they are and how they see the world. Philosopher Alain de Botton in "A Week at the Airport" notes, "If we were to spend a few days becoming aware of societies, the market, and ourselves, we would think more shrewdly, be confident in our choices, and far freer in our activities."

Travel doesn't necessitate lengthy stays on alien soil. It could be kitsch searching in a nearby town or a weekend adventure. A holiday is possible even in your own downtown region with a confined allowance and little time to get out of the house. With the abundance of choices, goals, aids, and logistics, the planning and preparation stages of travel can be a lot of enjoyment. Where do you begin the journey, how do you begin to journey, and where do you wish to go?

Budgeting and Finance: Managing finances is a major concern for any lifestyle, especially when traveling. For those living abroad for extended periods, such as six months in Mexico, there is a substantial and often unexpected economic commitment. Budgeting and financial preparedness will depend on lifestyle and any pending responsibilities in a foreign country. Short-term vacationing requires significantly less financial commitment than living in another country. A six-month commitment abroad necessitates careful financial planning. Each person should consider their own economic and financial situation before moving abroad.

Ways of Managing Finances while Living Abroad: Consulting a financial planner, accountant, or attorney to help manage your assets legally and judiciously while living abroad is a good financial strategy. Responsible financial management includes paying taxes, making investments, and regularly contributing to a retirement account. It is also advisable to carry some cash and credit to tide you over during any financial transition period. Most professionals will work with you via email or phone, especially if you are already a customer. You may also consider using a professional from a major city like Los Angeles who services your location.

Traveling Ex Tempore: There are two major costs associated with a vacation: travel and accommodations. For those who can experience budget travel without dipping into retirement savings, tickets are usually the largest cost. Look for off-season flights. In winter, head for a southern beach; in summer, escape to the north. The shoulder seasons are ideal as your vacation destination will still be warm, but you won't have to pay peak prices. Take advantage of low-cost accommodations and be flexible in terms of location and housing. The greatest savings often come from being open to new ideas. Set a travel budget and consider large fixed costs, such as rent, while also exercising smart economic management practices when budgeting your income and expenses.

CHAPTER 4

Cultural Immersion and Deep Connections

As a member of the human species, your senses are your primary tools for navigating the world. Sight, being the most prominent, allows you to quickly assess risks, identify resources for food, shelter, and warmth, and evaluate your environment. Touch helps you create and manipulate your surroundings, while hearing lets you discern the proximity and intentions of others. These senses are crucial for security and survival, aiding in communication and navigation.

However, when it comes to wanderlust, your senses serve more than just practical needs. Some individuals pursue something greater—less tangible but deeply felt. A connection with something new and different. Wanderlust provides a practical advantage beyond mere survival: the ability to communicate valuable information and foster trusted social bonds. Individual curiosity sparks knowledge, conversation, and creativity, leading to the development of new tools and methods. Sharing experiences and information beyond one's immediate community can benefit everyone. Simply wanting to share seemingly irrelevant details can bring peace through the revelation of shared experiences and common ground.

Local Interactions and Language Learning

Local interactions and language learning are critical for achieving deeper, more authentic connections during travel. Studies in tourism and travel research emphasize the importance of immersing oneself in another culture through interaction, language, first-hand experiences, and friendships. Lack of local interaction can lead to personal dissatisfaction and missed opportunities for growth. Language learning, particularly among the poorly-skilled, is a key barrier to local interaction and international education.

How often one travels or the time spent on a trip is a poor indicator of the value derived from the experience. The true value lies in the depth and diversity of the social and economic network built through local interactions. To make meaningful connections, one must know local words to make local friends and engage in face-to-face conversations that can change life paths. Language and personal interactions are what set travel apart from mere tourism.

Responsible Tourism

Responsible tourism involves travelers engaging in activities that provide direct and authentic encounters with local people, natural environments, and cultural heritage. This approach benefits both the traveler and the local community. Responsible tourism practices include:

- **Sustainability:** Using low-impact or vertically-focused organizations, adhering to leave-no-trace wilderness management rules, and carefully selecting trail routes and base camps to minimize environmental impact.
- **Local Resource Development:** Supporting initiatives like the Peace Corps, which trains volunteers to build on local heritage and finance the caretaking of historical and cultural resources. Adventure travel organizations also support native-

run eco-tourism programs, food co-ops, youth sports, and environmental education.

Travelers should seek to become part of the places they visit, contributing money and support to local areas while enriching their own lives. This approach allows travelers to pay fair market value for enhanced experiences and forge meaningful connections with local people, cultures, land, and wildlife. Responsible travel benefits both the traveler and the visited, often leading to personal transformation and a deeper appreciation for the world.

CHAPTER 5

Adventure and Bold Living

A dventure and bold living—if it doesn't come with at least some risk, it's not an adventure. Adventure, travel, and the joys of wanderlust are no longer seen as the hobby of those who can't get a real job or a way to pass the time before setting up a family. In fact, adventure can, does, and should help us all live more deeply, expand our comfort zones more fully, and interact with our world more completely. The wanderlust lifestyle is truly one of bold living. It is a life filled with passionate embraces, loud laughter, and the sincere pursuit of the world we love. However, the most bold and joyful lifestyle comes with challenges. The open road, leading everywhere and nowhere, in reality, takes us to the least visited places of the world, presenting countless challenges.

Risk: "Hours of boredom, moments of terror" - Risk is a key component of enjoying the joys found in wanderlust. While adventure and exploration are among the many joys of unprecedented wandering, much of what follows goes back to the basic principles of wandering discussed earlier. Adventure as transformation: our passions, pursuits, and choices are meant to push our boundaries, teach us about the world, and show us how much we love to laugh, how deeply to cry, and how constantly to embrace those whom we could not otherwise call friends. Passionate living—a life of adventure—is not a selfish one. By finding our own adventures, we reshape our personalities and often improve the world around us.

Risk-taking and Personal Growth

Risk-taking is a crucial aspect of personal growth, informing one's preferences and experiences. Travel often involves degrees of risk as individuals move beyond their borders and adopt various means of doing so. The fear or uncertainty of unfamiliar circumstances and the probable risks involved are linked to explorer travels as they push their comfort boundaries. For instance, the risk for someone who has never traveled to the Rocky Mountains is much higher than for those who regularly mountain bike through rocky terrains. Risk or challenge related to travel can be situational, but on average, those who spend their holidays exploring the Rocky Mountains face more risks than travelers who plan everything down to safe tourist resorts.

Embracing risk or crisis within choice is a primary tenet within the psycho-spiritual framework of growth and personal development. The wonder and awe arising from peak experience encounters generate responses and learning. Such strategies, incorporated into everyday life through encounters with nature as an expression of peak experience, aid personal development. It is possible to navigate changes or upheavals and emerge transformed more successfully when responding to risk-taking than without.

Within outdoor adventure tourism, and the lived experiences of the adventure-junky segment of the population, risk-taking promotes spatial, temporal, and cognitive expansion. Choices focused on risk-taking behaviors foster art within the participant and promote overall intellectual curiosity and complexity. Many engage in travel for holistic personal development, with a significant component being the acquisition of new perspectives, practices, and routines. The major appeal of travel is the experience of enlightenment or personal growth, closely correlated with recognition and awe. Travelers make such commitments when considering travel and choosing to undertake a journey. Management consultants Pam Goldsmith and Garry Waldorf, through their book *The Acme Whistle*, support this concept. The British law firm Clifford Chance leads renewed staff members on treks around London's Rubicon and through the engine room of the Magna Carta. These walks attempt to recreate the situations faced by genuine emigrants who had to step away from family infrastructure to create a new start. Mastering such difficult walks requires participants to leave London at five in the morning, wade through chest-high waters, and scale walls. Plans that are wishfully bold and smart form the core of wanderlust. Embracing the aesthetic of travel requires bold plans, vision, and strategy.

Pushing Comfort Zones

Comfort zones represent the barrier between what you already know and can do and what you cannot. Stepping outside these bounds entails inherent difficulties, but the question of whether it is worthwhile remains unwavering. Not only is it worthwhile, but it is also the sole route to personal growth and transformation. Every technological and medical breakthrough originated outside the comfort zone, and every job you abhorred eventually led you to your dream position. Understanding these truths outlines how pushing comfort zones truly pays dividends.

Breaking from routines and predetermined paths fosters growth. Heightened creativity, empathy, and sensitivity to people and ideas emerge as byproducts of stepping into the wild. Dabbling doesn't cut it; jumping into a small foot of foreign water leaves signs of growth obscure. However, leaping into unknown oceans tips over the horizon a multitude of skills and knowledge. Growth necessitates startlingly difficult and alarming experiences. These seemingly negative outcomes symbolize transformational confrontations breaking your comfort zones. This is the reality of pushing comfort zones: bold living. Smart travelers discover, through the wonder of wanderlust, that adversities develop the strength to embrace a better version of oneself.

CHAPTER 6

Sustainable Travel Practices

E nvironmentally friendly and people-supporting strategies are crucial for responsible travel. In this part, you will learn how to travel the world in a way that leaves it unharmed and supports the local people you meet along the way.

Why It Matters

In the first part of this chapter, we delved into the concept of wanderlust. Travelers seek deeper, more intimate, and real experiences of life, no matter the destination. However, those who write about the meaning, purpose, and path of travel often overlook the Earth's millions of people and the planet itself. In a world brimming with cultural diversity, many travelers put little thought into encounters with the inhabitants of the towns and villages they visit. Their worries lie with seeing the pyramids, climbing Everest, or finding the lions of Chobe, without considering the impact of their travels on local communities or the environment.

Mission to Wonder: Conscious travel excludes any and all exploitative travel. We assert our commitment to sustainability and connection with the places, cultures, and people we encounter. We hope our travel philosophy will transform the way we all travel in small but meaningful ways.

Eco-conscious Choices

Wanderlust urges travelers to expand their horizons, take endeavors beyond their comfort zones, and open themselves up to new mindsets and experiences. In a world widely accessible through technologies like air travel, maritime cruises, and overnight trains, this has substantial impacts on the environment. According to Husserl, "It is by traveling that a person puts creativity and spontaneity first in his life." Yet, irresponsible planet stewardship and the prioritization of commercial interests over natural resources have led many activists and scientists to criticize travel industries for the negative effects of mass displacement.

Traveling has the potential to educate travelers, open their worldviews, and build empathy and active solidarity with local communities. To minimize its impact, it is important to make environmentally conscious decisions.

From Fable and Fahnestock's perspectives, eco-conscious or sustainable tourists tend to shy away from popular, overcrowded areas and impromptu, short-term travel ideas to reduce their environmental impact. Sustainable tourists perceive environmental depletion as a major adverse influence of the tourist industry and appreciate preservation initiatives that minimize environmental impact. Active travelers who request detailed information about health and welfare utilize it to make environmentally conscious travel plans.

Eco-tourists often seek less-crowded and unique destinations to reduce their ecological footprint and embrace a more sustainable way of traveling. National media channels, travel books, and promotional material offer recommendations for discovering unique personal experiences across the globe.

Supporting Local Communities

Engaging ethically with locals transforms travel experiences. When travelers invest in travel experiences that teach them new skills or offer tours from locals, they connect deeply with the people and places they visit. This ethical engagement ensures that not only the powerful groups benefit but also the true stewards of the land and culture—those who responsibly sustain and share their stories and experiences.

Participating in local events and tours ensures that tourism dollars go directly to local families in the form of tips and sales. When small communities see tourism dollars coming in because of unique and authentic interactions, they are more likely to continue sharing their culture.

Helping others creates a community of connection that can lead to evolution from poverty. Engaging with locals means your tourism dollars will support them directly. Resorts and Safari camps that tout community engagement and give back are critical, but there is something powerful about direct individual-to-community giving. By truly engaging with local people, you can get far more in return.

CHAPTER 7

Digital Nomadism and Remote Work

Digital nomadism is a rapidly growing trend and can be seen as an extension of the indie traveler movement. It describes people who enjoy traveling, exploring new places, and taking advantage of location independence to change their surroundings often. If you are a mobile and tech-savvy professional—a designer, programmer, writer, internet marketer, blogger, or someone working in a business that can be done over the internet—you are a digital nomad. Many digital nomads share their stories on blogs, and some even make money by teaching others how to become digital nomads. Blogs and websites dedicated to this lifestyle are more popular than ever. You can work remotely while exploring and traveling the world, although it involves a lifestyle adjustment and a hands-on approach to finding remote work opportunities.

Tools and Resources

With a clear understanding of wanderlust and the popular approaches to remote work, it's time to get practical and explore specific tools and resources to make location independence a reality. This section covers a range of technologies and services to help aspiring digital nomads or remote workers blend productivity with adventure to realize their travel dreams. We also address the ethical and social dilemmas of digital nomadism and the global challenges posed by the "new colonialism" of Western digital commuters in low-cost environments. Appropriate legal and administrative frameworks are necessary to support this movement.

Essential Tools and Resources:

1. **A Blog/Website:** Share your experiences and expertise.
2. **Social Media:** Use platforms like Twitter, Facebook, LinkedIn, and others to connect with potential clients.
3. **Work Exchange Platforms:** Sign up for sites like Workaway and WWOOF to offer your time in exchange for room and board.
4. **Job Sites:** Explore job boards and websites that cater specifically to digital nomads, such as RemotelyAwesomeJobs, Work At My Desk, and RemoteOK. The job sections of Carbonmade and Behance are also worth checking out.
5. **Networking:** Making lots of friends is essential for growing your network and expanding your client base. This will also enhance your travel opportunities and potentially save money by staying with friends you make along the way.

Capabilities and Skills for Digital Nomadism:

- **Self-Discipline:** Maintain focus and productivity.
- **Time Management:** Balance work and travel effectively.
- **Intrinsic Motivation:** Stay motivated and driven.
- **Adaptability:** Navigate change and uncertainty with ease.

Practical Tools:

- **Communications:** Tools like Slack, Zoom, and Skype for effective communication.
- **Synchronization:** Platforms like Google Drive and Dropbox for file sharing and collaboration.
- **Correspondence:** Email management tools like Gmail and Outlook.
- **Office Administration:** Tools like Trello and Asana for project management.
- **Information and Transportation:** Apps like Rome2rio and Skyscanner for travel planning.
- **Social Bookings:** Platforms like Airbnb and Couchsurfing for accommodations.
- **Remote Professional Services:** Websites like Upwork and Fiverr for finding freelance work.

Work-Life Balance

While work is important and fulfilling for most digital nomads, it is not the only thing in life. Achieving a harmonious integration of work with personal leave and pleasure is crucial. Work-life balance describes the relationship between work and other life commitments and how they impact one another.

Understanding Work-Life Balance:

- It is not about scheduling an equal number of hours for work and leisure but about making work fit your lifestyle.
- It is the state of equilibrium where career and ambition are equally prioritized with leisure activities and family life.

Benefits of Work-Life Balance:

- Reduces stress and burnout.

- Improves overall well-being and happiness.
- Enhances productivity and creativity.

Strategies for Achieving Work-Life Balance:

- **Set Boundaries:** Define clear working hours and stick to them.
- **Prioritize Tasks:** Focus on high-priority tasks and delegate or eliminate low-priority ones.
- **Take Breaks:** Regular breaks improve focus and productivity.
- **Pursue Hobbies:** Engage in activities that bring joy and relaxation.
- **Stay Connected:** Maintain relationships with family and friends.

Some people believe that achieving something extraordinary requires choosing between a career and rest. However, this does not contribute to self-realization. A balanced path in life is essential. Focusing only on work or only on oneself can lead to stagnation and regrets later in life.

CHAPTER 8

Solo Travel and Group Dynamics

Solo travel, although not as common as communal travel, has attracted much media attention over the last couple of decades. Increasing news outlets highlight stories of individuals who conquer their fears of uncertainty and embrace their curiosity to travel alone. While not as popular as communal travel, solo travel is common, especially among female travelers. The underlying motivation is to gain autonomy, tranquility, and self-discovery. Moreover, solo traveling can alleviate one from the hassle of consensus building and increase sociability. The great variety and instances of solo travel suggest that it is an influential construct that leads individuals to travel in an alternative fashion.

Only a limited number of studies have attempted to explore solo traveling experiences. Therefore, a comprehensive literature review dedicated to the exploration of solo travelers is executed. Current trends within the solo travel segment, reasons why individuals travel solo, and the benefits and barriers are presented.

Group Dynamics in Leisure Travel

In group research, the dynamics of group relationships and experiences have grown. The United Nations World Tourism Organization (UNWTO) estimates that approximately 80% of travelers vacation with one or two others. Partners in travel are most often friends, followed by family. Generally, group research is fragmented, but there is an increasing appreciation for group research in leisure and tourism. Such studies assess communication, decision-making, influence, relationship, and member dynamics in families, couples, and peer groups. Some of these studies also address travelers in terms of cultural groups, travel industry work teams, volunteers, or government-sponsored cultural exchanges. Group travel brings group dynamics into markets, and more attention can be given to this research domain.

Benefits and Challenges
Benefits

Independent Adventure: "One is the loneliest number," according to the Harry Nilsson song, but not when it comes to exploring unfamiliar places and cultures and making new friends. According to the U.S. Travel Association, 80 percent of American travelers prefer to travel with a companion, but those intrepid loners who hit the road often enjoy surprising comfort and fun. By opting to go alone, a traveler has the freedom to build a trip around specific interests—be it exploring the world of folk music in Nashville or discovering Victorian cemeteries and crypts in London. Solo trips are full of happy surprises and offer excellent opportunities for introspection, rebuilding confidence, and making friends.

Getting Cozy: Travel ceases to be only about the destination when friends or family join the journey. Everyone loves a group of curious folk who want to hit the road together, plan a wedding or honeymoon trip, enjoy time with loved ones, or embark on a faith-based trip that involves prayer and good works. Sometimes, when on a research trip, publishers or others may travel with you, providing an engaging look at your work. These shared experiences can lead to fast friendships and lasting memories.

Challenges

Solo Travel: Traveling alone can come with challenges, such as feelings of loneliness or safety concerns. However, overcoming these challenges can lead to personal growth and a sense of empowerment.

Group Travel: Traveling with others requires compromise and consensus-building. Group dynamics can be challenging, with differing opinions and preferences that need to be managed.

Building Connections on the Road

Solo travel offers many opportunities for meeting other travelers and locals. It also provides an opportunity to connect inwardly, accompanied by shifts in values and lifestyle that call for openness to new experiences, flexibility, and a willingness to reexamine assumptions about destiny, success, and personal responsibility. Whether traveling alone or with a companion, you can increase your chances of striking up meaningful conversations with locals and fellow travelers.

The attraction of the road is especially strong among twenty- and thirty-somethings. Other ways to emphasize contact with other travelers include joining group tours, staying in hostels, or participating in local events. Passive travelers are more likely to experience chance meetings and spread out a network of contacts. Proactive efforts to make acquaintances can speed up the process, requiring a conscious effort to break out of a shell of privacy or reserve. Sitting alone at a restaurant table can provide more chances to make friends. Retirees or "trust fund" vagabonds may be more hesitant, feeling they are intruding into the company of others.

CHAPTER 9

Traveling with Purpose

W hen we travel with a purpose, we humanize our experiences. Whether we set out to volunteer, work, or simply find a better way to know the communities of a new place, gratification is generative. We know this from our own experiences of altruism and community service, from research on family cohesion at Rocky Mountain Fiddle Camp, and from studies of mature travelers who engage in educational travel or lifelong learning. Here, we review principles of successful programs propagated by Road Scholar and Emerging Horizons and reflect on the quest for human connection as proposed by commercial guides such as Lonely Planet.

Being intentionally on the road broadens our freedom because it extends beyond selfish behavior and opens the door to the kinds of connections we deeply desire. This is true on our home turf and even more so when we step through the threshold of known familiarity. By choosing to go global, we draw ourselves into ever-widening circles of shared experience with our common human community. The places you are preparing to visit are unique, valuable, and necessary parts of this community. We reach out to show our gratitude, appreciation, concern, love, and care during this process of discovery. The spiritual tradition we root ourselves in offers this as a starting place for others to embrace our boundless curiosity to see the world. We hope to inspire you to a broader, deeply insightful, critical appreciation of not only the world you live in but also the hospitality so many others are eager to show you during your travels.

Volunteering and Giving Back

Some prefer to seek work wherever they go. Job titles of digital nomads are as diverse as their home bases. For example, an opera singer working as a nanny in Geneva found opera jobs hard to come by and wanted to work on her languages. She discovered the office of Red Cross International across the street from where she worked and walked in to volunteer. They had an old computer and nothing for her to do, but she remembered some people she met there, bound to wheelchairs, had injuries that kept them in hospitals for years in their home countries. "So I tell them to send me wheelchairs so we can keep them there," said her office supervisor in charge of shipping. "So now that's my summer job. I pack and ship wheelchair parts to war-torn countries."

Volunteering can be more than just homestays. In an article on the type of travel experiences offered by Russian Life magazine, Nancy Ries, an associate professor and chair of anthropology at Colgate University, writes about an American who travels to Russia to visit children's camps. "His vacation," Ries explains, "is anything but a 'break' from work. His travel is seen as a form of worker pilgrimage as he enters this world through his service." Ries has written a fascinating series of articles discussing what she calls "refuge tourism," or traveling to war-torn regions, thin places, "as the orthodox describe them, the movement of the incense from the altar to the faithful and then back again."

Educational and Learning Opportunities

Whether on a solo journey or a family adventure, any traveler encounters myriad learning opportunities. By deliberately seizing these opportunities, individuals can grow vastly in terms of personal norms and values, intellectual understandings, cultural insights, and defined abilities and skills. Learning opportunities can be categorized as follows: (1) Modes of Travel, (2) Places to Visit, (3) Cultural Interactions, (4) Major Festivities and Events, and (5) Others. Travelers can engage in endless learning while spending time volunteering in diverse areas of their host community, such as in schools, where they can impart literacy or social education to local people in another language, or while studying Tai Chi, yoga, farming, or cooking.

The educational experience provided by various travel perspectives might be of tremendous importance for personal advancement and cultural interaction. Tourist guides, orientations, or tips related to places to visit or events to attend can substantially contribute to a successful and enjoyable tourist-educator experience. By participating in such activities and viewing things from the inside, travelers can develop practical work abilities as teachers, group and event managers, chefs, diet planners, and farmers to some extent. By constantly integrating local residents and other tourists, learners can develop their understanding of diversity, cross-cultural love, unity, and cooperation. In brief, one can grow considerably in terms of ability, integrity, and wisdom during a spectacular journey, becoming a global citizen or a person of substance.

CHAPTER 10

Health and Wellness on the Road

While traveling, it's crucial to keep health and wellness at the forefront of our minds. This chapter explores various aspects of maintaining health and wellness while on the road. Here, readers will learn how to approach exercise, stretching, and yoga while traveling, and how to prioritize time for meditative and spiritual practices. Topics of discussion include food and dietary considerations, new, natural, and alternative therapies, the nature of pests, infestations, poisons, and medications, dealing with tropical climates and surviving heat and sunshine, safety and prevention of theft, self-defense, and strategies for mental, emotional, and attitudinal wellness.

The concept of healthy living should encompass lifestyle patterns that can be followed regardless of location. Active people around the world tend to be healthier than their inactive counterparts, assuming they are not overfed. The best practices not only get and keep your body moving but also inspire unity, shelter, fitness, balance, inner silence, spiritual peace, courage, heightened awareness, perspective, joy, and gratitude. Healthy travelers can train, stretch, work out, or simply walk everywhere they go. They can practice yoga or meditation, or metta bhavana (loving-kindness meditation). They can connect with like-minded individuals in person or online. They can opt for healthier vehicles, roads, trails, light, air, landmarks, and accommodations. They can avoid unnecessary workloads, not engage in negative behaviors, and talk and listen to people who live with the same courage.

Physical and Mental Well-being

Traveling presents various risks and health challenges such as wildlife encounters, malaria, dengue fever, lost luggage, unexplained illnesses, parasites, ticks, animal attacks, local drivers, pickpockets, violent crimes, political instability, air pollution, passenger rights, car crashes, conflict, train disruptions, government red tape, refugee health, healthcare in different countries, and visa applications. Sensible precautions and acquired knowledge can reduce the fear of the unknown and foster a resilient mindset during travel.

Self-care Strategy:

- Listen to your body's needs and rest when necessary.
- Cultivate mental and physical toughness.
- Consider travel or medical insurance to cover unexpected travel difficulties.
- Maintain a sense of humor and avoid overreacting to risky situations.

Healthy Eating and Exercise

Travel often disrupts established habits, including eating a balanced diet and exercising regularly. When traveling, especially to locations with limited kitchen facilities, it's essential to adopt a pragmatic and adaptable approach to nutrition and physical activity.

Healthy Eating Tips:

- **Good Nutrition:** Focus on food that satisfies your body's needs, with a healthy mix of macronutrients, avoiding nutritionally empty foods like sugary snacks and fried foods.
- **Fresh Fruit:** Accessible and can be carried without spoiling.
- **Nuts:** Easy to carry, long-lasting, and good for various weather conditions.
- **Milk/Soya/Juice:** Fundamental for quick nutrition.
- **Chocolate/Sweet Bar:** Helpful for a short blood sugar drop.
- **Practical Approach:** Fill in other food groups as time and circumstances allow, without stress.

Exercise Tips:

- **Walking Tours:** Paris is great for walking tours, Tokyo is ideal for stretching.
- **Portable Exercise Equipment:** Jump ropes, resistance bands, and travel barbells are easy to carry.
- **Exercise Sample Cards:** Personal trainers often provide exercise cards with instructions for clients to follow while traveling.

Adopting these practical and adaptable strategies ensures you maintain your physical and mental well-being while exploring the world.

CHAPTER 11

Capturing Memories and Storytelling

In many ways, success in sharing a personal travel narrative can be heavily influenced by how we share those special moments with others. While some travelers may fancy themselves photographers and others may loathe the thought of carrying around an expensive camera or photo-taking device during their journey, capturing travel memories doesn't always have to involve a camera.

For some, journaling might seem obsolete in the age of digital devices and social media. However, there's something profound about travelers who find solace in jotting things down on paper. For many, it's about finding their voice. By moving beyond bullet-point thoughts and curating their daily activities, travelers can document their internal emotional states. Photography is also a form of journaling. Some people may not want to journal, and that's okay. When capturing your thoughts is not a priority, and you're in the moment of a stunning sunrise in the Italian countryside or taking in the silhouette of Utah's Delicate Arch, pulling out a camera, phone, or Polaroid can help you capture the moment for later reflection. Even if you don't care now, someone might. For Mother Nature's sake, capturing a special moment in time can create a long-lasting impact.

Photography and Journaling

Photography and Journaling: These are two of the most accessible tools for capturing travel memories. For over a century, photography has been a popular form of preservation. It's all about how you use it. Many of us use photography for memento value—such as a picture of you in front of the Eiffel Tower with loved ones to remember a trip to Paris. While this is quite right and innocent, the kind of photography I suggest delves deeper into the experience—turning a casual vacation into a unique piece of memoir.

Journaling: This precedes photography and is a written form of the same principle. Based on experience design, our journals—logbooks, scrapbooks, travelogues—can evolve from mere lists of to-dos to reflections, narratives, and strong personal storytelling. This transforms travel from mainstream to official.

Photography Tips:

- **Document Experiences:** Beyond standard photographs of must-visits, take pictures capturing experiences and people. Seek instances where a story needs to exist: a tender love story unfolding at a Paris café, the wind in your hair atop a rollercoaster, or an overwhelmed soul standing at the base of an enormous monument.

- **Quality over Quantity:** Modern digicams and mobile phone cameras take excellent quality pictures. Unlike old days with limited prints per shot, now you can click as many times as needed until you get it right. There's always a delete button to free unwanted space.

- **Candid Shots:** Take candid shots of ordinary people doing their daily routines. Convince strangers for a portrait. Multiple photos in sync can show variations in motion. Unlike old-school photography, you don't have to wait for days to get prints.

Journaling Tips:

- **Reflection and Narration:** Go beyond to-do lists to reflection and narrative forms of documentation. Transform your travel log into a personal storytelling masterpiece.
- **Combining Photography and Journaling:** Attach prints to your journal entries. Write reflections on captured pictures to create a rich travel memoir.

Sharing Experiences with Others

Sharing experiences with others allows travelers to take their wanderlust experiences and share them meaningfully. As layered meanings, engaging personal stories, and social sharing deepen, expressing and communicating wanderlust makes connections more real. This could be useful for team-building or offline instructing, encouraging participants to share an experience with a stranger or an acquaintance who can appreciate theirs.

Exploration of this section reveals how travel stories resonate with others, inspiring fellow wanderers and engaging people on their journeys through shared stories. This section helps recognize shared experiences brought up in stories. People might prompt original engagement with future or alternative ways of networking based on the energy that emerges from shared stories. Remember to share why you feel the need for these stories with participants, so the concept remains with them throughout. To foster a sense of community, the feeling of belonging to a greater whole can be included, stemming from our adventurous sparks that drive us to engage on social sharing websites. Together, our stories and interests weave a narrative of "togetherness" and initiate social sharing.

CHAPTER 12

Reflections on Wanderlust and Personal Growth

As our semester nears its close, we have taken time to reflect on the concept of wanderlust and how travel has contributed to our individual growth. The experiences shared continue to shape our present aspirations and outlooks on the world, echoing the wonder of our first day in Europe. Many of us, avid readers who believed that studying abroad would be life-changing, never fully expected to become the versions of ourselves we are today, having become world travelers. Throughout the semester, our capacity for introspection deepened as we grappled with the challenges of forming relationships and finding ourselves in changing environments. Before sharing our final thoughts, we will discuss our aspirations for the future. By connecting with others in foreign spaces and reconnecting with ourselves through solitude, we have discovered the qualities we most esteem. Several of us wish to focus on personal growth and maximize our potential in the coming year. While discussing our favorite parts of the semester, we often mention monuments and landmarks in passing but reflect greatly on the deep and true connections made with new friends.

These reflections help us move beyond merely dealing with practicalities to connect with living deeply and soulfully. As our journeys abroad come to a close, we hope to carry forward attitudes rife with hope and knowledge: "Carry forward what you have learned through your unique experience, with adaptations to your personal lifestyle and thought utilities." While studying in London, several of us were asked what we planned to do upon returning to the United States. Though each response varied, they all included the ideals of "bettering" and "improving." We now know that our experiences have significantly widened our perspectives and worlds. We may have traversed the physical landscapes of Western Europe, but even more so, we have explored the terrain of our own lives, dreams, and aspirations. By leaving our footprints in different cities, we return home feeling full in our hearts, ripe with shared experiences and a network of forever friends. Our journeys led us to meet many other young travelers on the same paths of self-discovery and bold living, each of us wandering to uncover our most desired "way."

Lessons Learned and Future Aspirations

Wanderlust, as an ambiguous human condition, is substantial to young people who have dedicated significant time and energy to traveling. It is a major dimension of agentic potential in forging a new identity. Providers such as volunteers or language schools have figured out ways to profit by offering spaces for personal, few-boundary incentive mechanisms to manifest. However, professional or consumerized host organizations are generally not the authors of what truly happens abroad when independent travelers and wanderlusters are on the road. It is unique for individuals to pinpoint the circumstances, experiences, and people they connect with. From my data, it is clear that independent travel experiences in various countries—where currency, language, and norms of behavior change—are among the most astonishing and moving reports.

Many encounters are casual, occurring frequently, but travel itself is unique. Given that young people between 18 and 34 are heavy participants in international travel and experience, and that older age groups are likely to initiate travel with enough experience, wanderlust broadens and deepens our connections and choices. It helps open our eyes, expanding options even when undesirable or unpleasant. Tour excursions often lead to revisiting home with alternative routes, providing new perspectives on one's life path.

Integration of Travel Experiences into Daily Life

Just as dreaming helps us mull over recent experiences and solve problems, longing for adventure can spur us to plan the next trip and reflect on how to infuse life with the values we experience on the road. While only a small number of people from rich countries undertake major volunteer projects, millions volunteer in smaller ways while traveling—painting homes and schools, constructing sidewalks, rebuilding after disasters. The point of these projects is not what is built but the interaction with strangers and the feeling of working for something greater than personal pleasure, such as helping a struggling community recover from a disaster.

Some people volunteer to help animals, assist in schools and clinics, or work on environmental projects. Travelers volunteer to learn from deprived, rural Australians, or participate in events like music festivals. Doing what might seem like a hybrid of extreme experiences, uncomfortable tasks, and the buzz of travel integrates experiential aspects into life overall. Many may avoid such journeys, assuming the benefits stay abroad rather than continuing to impact their everyday existence upon returning home.

www.ingramcontent.com/pod-product-compliance
Ingram Content Group UK Ltd.
Pitfield, Milton Keynes, MK11 3LW, UK
UKHW031031171224
452675UK00006B/695